D1511888

Antoine Sicotte
The Rebel Chef

Photographer: Albert Elbilia
Art director: Albert Elbilia
Book design and layout: Albert Elbilia, Antoine Sicotte and Antoine Ross Trempe
Culinary consultant: Éric Régimbald
Photography assistant: Stéphane Losq
Graphic designers: Marylin Deguire and Gabrielle Godbout
English translator: Lorien Jones

Project editor: Antoine Ross Trempe

The publisher acknowledges the financial support of the Government of Canada through the Canada Book Fund (CBF) for its publishing activities and the support of the Government of Quebec through the tax credits for book publishing program (SODEC).

ISBN 978-2-920943-70-4

Legal Deposit: 2014
Bibliothèque et Archives du Québec
Library and Archives Canada

Printed in Canada

Antoine Sicotte

THE REBEL CHEF

For my two little dumplings, Lili and Giselle.
I hope you learn to love food as much as I do.

Antoine Sicotte

THE REBEL CHEF

Antoine Sicotte

Preface by Gilbert Sicotte
Photography by Albert Elbilia

cardinal

Chinatown

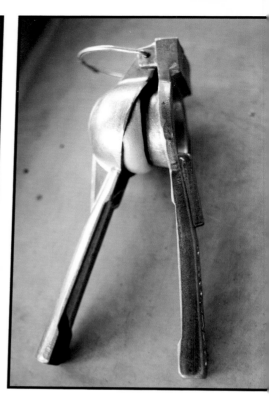

Preface

When I was a young lad and in school, I always went home for lunch. I remember dreaming, during my walk, of the heavenly aroma that would greet me at the door: roasting onions for my mother's *pâté chinois*, the Quebecois version of shepherd's pie, made from that Sunday's roast beef and gravy. It was inviting, comforting, full of love. In our house, the family meal reigned supreme. On Saturday mornings as a teenager, I'd lounge around in bed for a while before getting up, trying to guess what my mother was making down in the kitchen by inhaling the delectable scents floating up to my bedroom; Saturday was the day she would do all her baking and stewing for the rest of the week.

So it pleases me to think that perhaps my son, Antoine, enjoyed playing this guessing game as much as I did on those lazy Saturday mornings, when, as a father, I would get up early to whip up a batch of my Bolognese sauce, stroganoff crêpes, or fudgy Marguerite cake. Because I know that my son, the successful musician I'm so very proud of, also treasures the time he spends cooking for his own family. And he calls himself a rebel!

Gilbert Sicotte

MEETING THE REBEL CHEF

I'll admit, I wasn't exactly sure where to start with this foreword. How do you describe a guy like The Rebel Chef in just a few pages? How would our meetings pan out? Turns out, I had nothing to worry about; right off the bat, he decided that we would meet up at his place and just roll with it. No agenda, no formalities. "Plus, we'll be more relaxed here than at a café or a restaurant," he told me. The plan was simple, really: a casual, no-holds-barred *tête-à-tête* to really get to know the Rebel Chef. I had prepared a few ideas to guide us, but in the end the conversation flowed without a hitch, and before I knew it, hours had rocketed by. There we were in his family room, a space jumping with personality, dominated by oranges and reds, the walls bordered and hung with musical instruments that seemed to sprout right out of the walls. If it had been anyone else's house I would've felt intimidated, but with him, I wasn't. He spoke clearly and animatedly, expressing endless curiosity and radiating unstoppable energy about every subject we broached. This was his opportunity to speak from the heart about what is, for him, a true passion. To describe the experience in a nutshell: Antoine Sicotte (aka The Rebel Chef) got right down to it and gave up the goods, the step-by-step story of his journey from the studio to the kitchen.

NOT YOUR TYPICAL TEENAGER

Antoine looks back on his days as a fledgling cook with bittersweetly nostalgic stars in his eyes: "I was around 11, my parents had just split up, and cooking was a bonding mechanism for me and my dad. It's what really brought us close. He had no idea what he was doing in the kitchen, he was on his own, and so we learned as a team. The weekends he had my brother, my sister, and me are forever stamped in my memory, and so are the dishes we made together."

From the time he hit his teens, though, Antoine's world revolved around music. "I picked up the bass because, honestly, an instrument with only four strings seemed way easier to play than a guitar! When I was thirteen, my band would practice at the neighborhood youth center and that's how I was really able to nurture my love of music." Initially influenced by "cerebral" music—like prog rock and jazz (Rush, Uzeb, and Chick Corea)—his tastes gradually evolved to a more melodic, heartfelt style that came from a deeper place, and he discovered artists like Lou Reed, Miles Davis, and The Rolling Stones. This new musical epiphany cemented the path he was eventually destined to follow. "My quest for minimalism and pure melody in my music also applies to the way I cook. For me, choosing simple, quality ingredients, and allowing their true flavors to really shine, are far more important than fussy techniques and complicated preparations."

"FOR ME, CHOOSING SIMPLE, QUALITY INGREDIENTS, AND ALLOWING THEIR TRUE FLAVORS TO REALLY SHINE, ARE FAR MORE IMPORTANT THAN COMPLICATED TECHNIQUES AND PREPARATIONS."

Antoine had always had a hunch that higher education just wasn't in the cards for him, so he left high school to earn a living and figure out what he wanted to do with his life. His drive to create music won out: he taught himself to play the guitar, joining several bands and experimenting with different musical styles. This wasn't just a hobby. After spending a few years working in restaurants, Antoine enrolled in a sound engineering program in Montreal, and there, a light bulb went off. "I learned how music worked from the inside out, and that was it for me!" In 1993, while in school, he met James Renald, who would become his partner in music; the meeting would change the course of his career. Antoine and James clicked instantly, and they soon started writing together as Sky. When I asked him how they came up with the name, he burst out laughing and said, "Well, we actually didn't really spend much time on the name. We saw some graffiti in a really nasty back alley and we realized that, design-wise, the name had style. It was just punchy."

THE RISE TO FAME

Sky released its debut, self-produced album in 1997, on the duo's own label, Phat Royal. After a memorable gig for industry bigwigs, the guys signed their first major label deal. Antoine and James then travelled to New York and Toronto to record their sophomore album, *Piece of Paradise*. Its 1999 release was a turning point in Antoine's career, and in 2000, the group was awarded the Juno (Canada's equivalent to the Grammys) for Best New Artist. The band achieved international success with this album, and toured the world. "This was when we were really living the rock star lifestyle: fancy hotels, studios in L.A., collaborations with amazing musicians…"

"THIS WAS WHEN WE WERE REALLY LIVING THE ROCK STAR LIFESTYLE: FANCY HOTELS, STUDIOS IN L.A., COLLABORATIONS WITH AMAZING MUSICIANS…"

FROM STUDIO TO KITCHEN

When the group finally parted ways, there was no way Antoine was going to give up music. He continued to produce albums for various artists, collaborated as a producer, and kick-started a brand new band. He settled into family life, buying a home with his wife, Joé; little Lili was born in 2006, and his second daughter, Giselle, arrived in 2009, during the making of The Rebel Chef.

"FOR THE FIRST TIME IN MY LIFE, I HAD A PLACE TO ENJOY MY WORK AND SPEND TIME WITH MY FAMILY AND FRIENDS!"

Buying a house is what cinched Antoine's decision to pursue his passion for food. "For the first time in my life, I had a place to really enjoy working and hanging out with my family and friends." He started spending more and more time cooking, experimenting with flavors and testing out recipes of his own creation. He craved to learn, and fed his desire by devouring (not literally!) books on cuisine, meeting other foodies, honing and refining his skills, and just diving right in and getting his hands dirty, no matter what the results. His biggest discovery—and this was a big one—was that teaching yourself means there are no rules. "I wanted to revisit my favorite tried-and-true classics, but then add a rock 'n' roll twist by swapping ingredients or plating them in some crazy new way." Somehow, he also found the time to indulge his other passions: cigars (he has a collection worthy of Hugh Hefner), quality booze (especially calvados and rum), and fine wines (believe me, his wine cellar is a masterpiece!).

Antoine echoes his musical ethos in his cuisine by fusing different flavors (instead of melodies and rhythms), paying tribute to simple, yet delicious, ingredients, and, of course, always injecting a shot of chutzpah into the mix.

Silence in the studio!

Carpe noctem . . .

Antoine sees any time he cooks as an opportunity to get together with loved ones and celebrate life over a lip-smacking meal, with everyone gathering in the kitchen beforehand to talk and share a few laughs. He also knows that the preparation leading up to a meal promises just as much pleasure as the main event. Choosing (and ogling) delicious market-fresh ingredients, discovering enthusiastic and knowledgeable local vendors who are genuinely proud of their products and put their hearts into sourcing the highest-quality foods, and getting fired up about creating a memorable meal, are what transform meal planning from a chore into something magical.

"FOR ME, COOKING MEANS HANGING OUT WITH MY FAVORITE PEOPLE, HAVING A GOOD TIME, AND JUST ENJOYING LIFE."

Over the years, Antoine has done some serious entertaining, having people over a few times a week and creating eclectic menus for his guests, from more elaborate "haute cuisine"-type dishes to family-style, pass-around-the-table platters of pure comfort. "I have friends who are real foodies and always expect the very best, but I also have friends who are new to the whole game. I tried to keep both ends of the spectrum in mind when I developed my recipes so that everyone can enjoy them!"

AKA: THE REBEL

chef

A REBEL'S VISION

Antoine had been toying with the idea of writing a book for a while, but it wasn't until early 2008 that he actually began conceptualizing The Rebel Chef. Without losing sight of his philosophy that food can be full of flavor and still easy to prepare, he played around with different cookbook concepts. He wanted to create something different, halfway between a practical guide for home cooks and a gastronomic adventure. "I might not be a professionally-trained chef, but everything I learned, I learned myself by reading, travelling, and meeting others who are as passionate about food as I am. Anyone can do it." An avid cookbook collector himself, Antoine set out to design a colorful, inviting book—something that reflected his personality. "I've never been a fan of those frilly books with pages and pages of instructions; I wanted a book that was jam-packed with great ideas, but also a book that packs a punch design-wise, something that people are going to want to pick up and leaf through just because it looks awesome."

When setting out to write the recipes, it was impossible for Antoine to stick to just one style of cuisine. Being self-taught, he had the freedom to explore a chaotic mishmash of influences, hopping from Italy to Thailand, Jamaica to Japan to the Middle East to France. This book caters to every occasion imaginable, with dishes to cook on a Wednesday evening, to last-minute party nibbles, to tapas, desserts, and midnight snacks. Starting with a morning menu, the book glides into brunch, and then eases into lunch and dinner, ending with Antoine's favorite late-night nosh. "The idea was for this book to express the bright-eyed, sunny, family man part of my personality, but also to reveal my inner night owl, my rock 'n' roll side."

Table of Contents

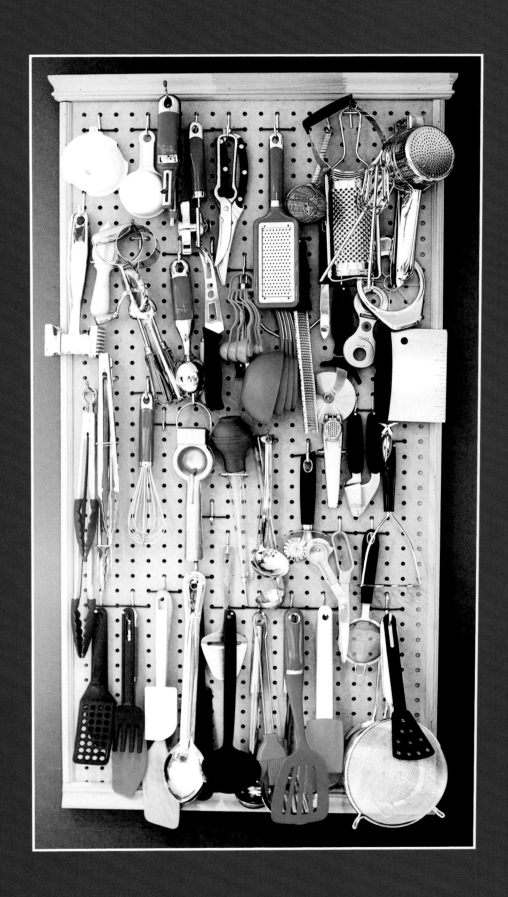

WARNING

THE TIMES PROVIDED IN THIS BOOK ARE FOR
INFORMATIONAL PURPOSES ONLY. PERSONS FOLLOWING
THE RECOMMENDATIONS OF THIS WORK DO SO UNDER
THEIR OWN RESPONSIBILITY.*

*OR JUST EAT WHATEVER YOU WANT, WHENEVER YOU WANT!

6AM / 11AM

ORANGE FLOWER BAKLAVA

NOTES FOR 16 SERVINGS

For the syrup:
1/2 cup maple syrup
A few drops lemon juice
1 tsp orange flower water
A few drops almond extract

For the baklava filling:
3 cups pitted dates
Zest from 1 small orange
A pinch of cinnamon
1/3 cup orange juice
3/4 cup sliced toasted almonds

For the pastry:
1 package phyllo pastry (1 lb/16 oz)
Melted butter

MUSIC

Preheat the oven to 350°F (175°C).
For the baklava filling: In a food processor, purée the dates, orange zest, cinnamon, and orange juice. Set aside. To assemble the baklava: With scissors, cut the phyllo pastry in half to make 2 rectangles, about 8 inches x 12 inches each. Brush 14 sheets of pastry with melted butter and place on a buttered baking sheet. Spread the date filling and 1/2 cup almonds over top. Place 14 more buttered phyllo sheets over the filling and brush the top generously with butter. Before putting the baklava in the oven, slice it into 24 triangles. Bake for 25 to 30 minutes, until the baklava is golden brown and crispy. While the baklava is baking, heat the maple syrup in the microwave, or on the stovetop. Add the lemon juice, orange flower water, and almond extract. Take the baklava out of the oven, pour the hot syrup over top, and sprinkle with the remaining almonds.

Caffè Miniveneziano, Caffè

Caffè ristretto,

Glassique

I love coffee...

Caffè lungo

corretto, Caffè

Caffè latte, Cappuccino, Caffè

Caffè Amalfi, Caffè macchiato, Caffè

Café Italia
Montreal

THE WORLD'S BEST
BANANA MUFFINS

NOTES FOR 12 HUGE MUFFINS

3/4 cup sour cream
1 tsp baking soda
1/2 cup butter
1 cup brown sugar
2 large eggs
1 tsp vanilla
3 very ripe (black) bananas, mashed
1 tsp baking powder
2 cups unbleached flour

MUSIC

Preheat the oven to 350°F (175°C).

In a small bowl, combine the sour cream and baking soda. Set aside. With a hand or stand mixer, cream together the butter and sugar for 5 minutes. Add the eggs, one at a time, and then add the vanilla. Mix well. Add the mashed bananas and the sour cream mixture. Combine the dry ingredients and add them to the liquid mixture. Pour this batter into the cups of a buttered muffin pan and bake for 18 to 20 minutes, or until a toothpick inserted into the center of a muffin comes out clean. Let the muffins cool on a baking rack.

Tip: For ultra-decadent muffins, add 3/4 cup white or dark chocolate chips to the batter before pouring it into the pan.

My wife whips up a batch of these muffins for every special occasion: she decorates them with colorful icing and candy for Halloween, Valentine's Day and the girls' birthdays. They flip out over them! But I like them best fresh out of the oven, slathered in butter,

or even chocolate hazelnut spread!

LILI'S OMELET

NOTES

3 eggs
1 tbsp sour cream
2 tbsp cheddar cheese (or any cheese of your choice), grated
1 shallot, thinly sliced
1 slice ham, chopped
1/4 cup red, orange, or yellow pepper, finely diced
2 mushrooms, finely diced
Salt and freshly ground pepper
1 tsp butter

MUSIC

In a bowl, combine all of the ingredients, except the butter. Heat the butter in a pan and cook the omelet for 5 minutes on each side.

Tip: Serve with 1 tbsp salsa (see recipe on page 086).

FOR 2 KIDS

lovely, lili!

SALMON CAVIAR CYLINDERS

NOTES FOR 4 SERVINGS

4 slices bread
1/2 lb (8 oz) smoked salmon
1 tbsp capers, chopped
1 tbsp red onion, chopped
1 tbsp lemon juice
Salt and freshly ground pepper
1/2 cup sour cream
2 English cucumbers, peeled and thinly sliced
1 small can (2 oz) caviar
2 tbsp olive oil
1 tsp lemon juice
Fresh dill or fennel fronds, chopped

MUSIC

For this recipe, you'll need a round stainless steel cookie cutter or cooking ring, about 2-1/2 inches in diameter. Toast the slices of bread and then use the cookie cutter to cut out 4 rounds. Finely chop the smoked salmon. In a bowl, combine the salmon, capers, red onion, and lemon juice. Season with a pinch of salt, and pepper to taste.

To assemble the stacks, place the cookie cutter in the center of a plate. Layer the ingredients in the cookie cutter by starting with a round of toast, and spread on a good spoonful of sour cream. Add 1/8 of the salmon mixture, some sliced cucumber, and 1 tsp caviar. Repeat with more sour cream, cucumber, and salmon. Lightly press the top of the stack to make sure the layers are packed together.

Carefully remove the cookie cutter and repeat the process to make 4 stacks. Combine the olive oil and lemon juice with the chopped fresh dill or fennel fronds. To serve, top each stack with 1/2 tsp caviar and drizzle a bit of the dressing over each.

... all year long.

STROGANOFF BUNDLES

| FOLDING CRÊPES | 101.1 | FIGURE 1.3 |

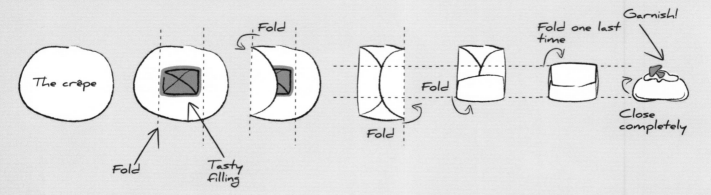

The crêpe

Fold

Tasty filling

Fold

Fold one last time

Garnish!

Fold

Fold

Close completely

NOTES FOR 4 SERVINGS

1 tbsp butter
3 large onions, sliced
1 tbsp sugar
1 tbsp butter
1/2 cup onions, thinly sliced
1 cup in-season mushrooms, sliced
1 lb (16 oz) ground beef
2 tbsp flour
1 tsp salt
1 tsp pepper
1 tsp paprika
1 can (10 oz) cream of mushroom soup
1 cup sour cream
8 small, thin crêpes
(store-bought, or from your favorite recipe)
2 tbsp melted butter

MUSIC

Preheat the oven to 350°F (175°C).

In a pan, melt the butter and add the 3 sliced onions. Cook the onions until they turn translucent and then add the sugar. Continue cooking for about 30 minutes over medium-low heat, until the onions are caramelized.

In another pan, heat the rest of the butter and sauté the 1/2 cup of thinly sliced onions with the mushrooms. Add the ground beef and break it apart with a spoon. Add the flour, salt, pepper, and paprika, and continue sautéing until the meat is fully cooked. Add the can of cream of mushroom soup (undiluted) and let the mixture simmer for 10 minutes. Add the sour cream at the very end and mix well.

I usually spoon about 1 tbsp of the stroganoff onto the center of each crêpe, fold them into little packets, brush them with melted butter, and cook them in the oven on a baking sheet for about 15 minutes (making sure to cook the packets seam side down so they don't open).

I like to serve them with the caramelized onions and a hefty scoop of sour cream. Perfect for Sunday brunch!

tip

This stroganoff will turn your kids into mushroom maniacs!

CHEESEBOARD & TOMATO TART

NOTES FOR 1 TART

1 store-bought or homemade pie crust, unbaked (preferably shortcrust pastry)
1 tbsp Dijon mustard
2 ripe tomatoes, thinly sliced
1 onion, thinly sliced
1 clove garlic, thinly sliced
1 cup cheese of your choice, grated or cut into small pieces (I usually make this when I've got a whack of cheese ends hanging around in the fridge. The older and stinkier, the better; just don't forget to slice off the moldy bits!)
Herbes de Provence to taste (or your favorite fresh, chopped herbs)

MUSIC

Preheat the oven to 350°F (175°C).
Brush the bottom of the crust with Dijon. Fan out the tomato and onion slices over the mustard, in alternate layers. Sprinkle the garlic over top and season with salt and pepper. Finish by adding the herbs and the cheese and bake for about 25 minutes, until the crust and cheese are golden brown. Serve with a nice green salad.

Tip: Perfect for an afternoon of fridge cleaning!

Serve these little flavor bombs for brunch or as an appetizer.

BACON-WRAPPED DATES

NOTES FOR 30 HORS D'OEUVRES

30 pitted dates
10 slices bacon, cut lengthwise into 3 strips each

MUSIC

Preheat the oven to 350°F (175°C).
Roll a thin strip of bacon around each date and secure them with toothpicks. Cook for 20 minutes, until the bacon is crispy.

11AM / 4PM

COUSTEAU SALAD

NOTES FOR 2 SERVINGS

8 oz octopus, cut into 1/2-inch pieces
1 cup sake
5 oz dried seaweed (wakame)
1 clove garlic, finely chopped
1 tbsp vegetable oil
2 small Lebanese cucumbers, julienned
1 carrot, julienned

For the vinaigrette:

1 oz fresh ginger, peeled and julienned
1/4 cup rice vinegar
2 tbsp vegetable oil
2 tbsp mirin
1 tbsp honey
1 tsp sesame oil
1 tsp fine salt

MUSIC

In a pot, simmer the octopus in the sake, covered, for 1 hour and 30 minutes. In a bowl, cover the seaweed with water and let it soak for 10 minutes. After 10 minutes, drain the seaweed, thinly slice it, and divide it between 2 bowls. Drain the octopus and briefly sauté it with the garlic in a bit of vegetable oil. For the vinaigrette, combine all the vinaigrette ingredients in a bowl. Divide the cucumbers, carrot, and the octopus between the 2 bowls and drizzle the vinaigrette over each salad. Serve immediately.

EGGPLANT CAVIAR AND GOAT CHEESE TOAST

NOTES FOR 30 APPETIZERS

1 large eggplant
Juice of 1 lemon
1/2 clove garlic, crushed
2 tbsp olive oil
Salt and freshly ground pepper
1 baguette, thinly sliced
A bit of olive oil
10 oz goat cheese with rind, sliced

MUSIC

Preheat the oven to 350°F (175°C).
Pierce the eggplant a few times with a fork and place on a baking sheet. Cook in the oven for about an hour, or until the flesh is soft and tender. Let the eggplant cool slightly and then slice it lengthwise and scoop out the flesh. If needed, drain the flesh beforehand to remove any excess liquid. In a food processor, purée the eggplant, lemon juice, garlic, and olive oil until smooth. Season with salt and pepper to taste. Brush the baguette slices with a bit of olive oil and toast in the oven until crispy and golden brown, about 5 minutes. Spread 1 tsp of the eggplant purée onto each toasted baguette slice and top with a slice of goat cheese. Broil in the oven, until the cheese starts to melt and becomes beautifully golden. Keep a close eye on them because they'll burn if you turn your back for too long!

Fresh **tomatoes**, canned tomatoes, tomato passata... I love them all!!

PASTA PUTTANESCA

NOTES FOR 4 SERVINGS

2 tbsp olive oil
2 cloves garlic, thinly sliced
1 dried piri-piri chili, crushed
1 can (28 oz) whole Italian tomatoes
1/2 cup anchovy-stuffed green olives (if you can find them), sliced
OR 1/2 cup pitted green olives, sliced, and 1/2 tbsp anchovy paste
1/2 cup black olives, sliced
1/2 cup caperberries, sliced
1 tbsp capers
16 oz (1 package) spaghetti

MUSIC

In a pan, heat the oil and sauté the garlic and pepper. When the garlic is golden, add the tomatoes and crush them with a spoon, directly in the pan. Reduce the heat to medium-low. Add the olives and the caperberries. Rinse the capers and add them to the sauce, and then let the sauce simmer for about 30 minutes. Cook the pasta in salted water, drain, and toss it with the sauce in a large, warmed bowl.

Tip: For some seriously rockin' pasta, top with shavings of fresh Parmesan and pair it with a nice bottle of red wine!

CHICKEN TIKKA

NOTES FOR 6 SERVINGS

1 tsp cumin seeds, toasted
1 tsp coriander seeds, toasted
1 cup plain yogurt
4 cloves garlic
1 inch fresh ginger, peeled and chopped
3 tbsp vegetable oil
2 tbsp lime juice
A pinch of salt
1 clove
1 tsp garam masala
A pinch of freshly ground pepper
A pinch of cayenne pepper
4 chicken breasts, cut into cubes (or strips)

MUSIC

In a food processor, combine all the ingredients, except for the chicken. When the spices are well-mixed, transfer the sauce to a plastic bag, or a bowl, and add the chicken. Let the chicken marinate for at least 4 hours. Preheat the barbecue to 400°F (200°C). Thread the marinated chicken onto skewers (ideally wooden and soaked in water for 30 minutes). Grill the chicken for 9 to 12 minutes, until cooked.

Tip: I like my chicken tikka with a side of sliced fresh mango sprinkled with toasted pink peppercorns and lime juice. It's seriously fantastic!

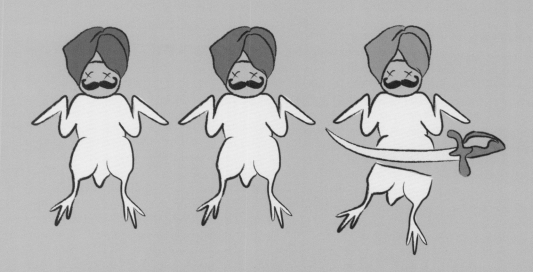

PIZZA TONINO

NOTES FOR ONE 12-INCH PIZZA

For the pizza dough:
1 packet (7 oz) yeast
3/4 cup warm water
2-1/2 cups all-purpose flour
1 tsp salt
1 tbsp olive oil

For the sauce:
1 can (28 oz) whole Italian tomatoes
2 tbsp olive oil
1 small dried hot pepper, crushed (or a pinch of crushed red pepper flakes)
1/4 cup fresh Parmesan cheese, grated
A pinch of dried oregano
1 tsp fennel seeds
A small spoonful of anchovy paste, or 1 anchovy fillet, chopped
1 tbsp capers, chopped

For the pizza toppings:
Cheese of your choice (mozzarella, Mozzarella di Bufala, goat cheese, provolone, etc.)
Any combination of:
Meat (pepperoni, sausage, prosciutto, capicollo, etc.)
Seafood (shrimp, scallops, squid, etc.)
Veggies (marinated artichoke hearts, spinach, onions, etc.)

MUSIC

Start by making the dough: combine the yeast and 3/4 cup warm water and let it sit for 10 minutes. After 10 minutes, combine the proofed yeast with 1 cup flour and the salt. Knead the dough for 5 minutes and then let it rest for 30 minutes, covered with a damp cloth. Add the rest of the flour and the olive oil and then knead for 5 minutes longer. Cover it again with the damp cloth, and let it rise for 1 hour and 30 minutes at room temperature. Meanwhile, prepare the sauce: Pour the tomatoes into a wire mesh strainer placed over a bowl, and cut the tomatoes open to drain the liquid. Transfer the tomatoes to another bowl and add the olive oil, hot pepper, Parmesan cheese, oregano, fennel seeds, anchovy paste, and capers. Mix well and set aside. To make the pizzas, preheat the oven to 450°F (230°C). Divide the pizza dough into two balls and flour a flat work surface. Roll out a ball of dough into a 12-inch circular crust, spread half of the sauce over top, and sprinkle with the cheese of your choice. Add your favorite toppings and then cook it on a preheated pizza stone (or, if you don't have one, on a pizza pan) for about 10 minutes, until the cheese is melted and the crust is crisp.

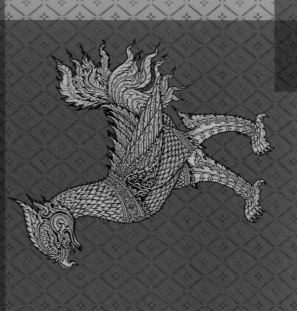

Rebel Thai Wrap

NOTES FOR 4 SERVINGS

1 pork loin, thinly sliced (about 1/4 inch per slice)
4 cups chicken stock
Rice vermicelli
1/2 cup crunchy peanut butter
2 tbsp rice vinegar
1 tbsp fish sauce (nuoc mam)
1/4 cup water
2 tbsp honey
1 tsp sambal oelek
A head of frisée lettuce, leaves washed and torn into pieces (big enough to make a small wrap, about 1-1/2 inches)
A few leaves fresh Thai basil
A couple of limes, cut into wedges

MUSIC

Poach the sliced pork in the chicken broth until it's fully cooked through, about 5 minutes. Set aside. Cook the vermicelli according to the package directions. Set aside. For the peanut sauce, combine the peanut butter, rice vinegar, fish sauce, water, honey, and sambal oelek in a bowl, mixing until the sauce is smooth. Set all of the ingredients on the table so that everyone can make their own wraps: just take a piece of lettuce and top it with a bit of vermicelli, a slice of pork, a spoonful of sauce, and a Thai basil leaf. Finish with a squeeze of lime, carefully roll up into wraps, and enjoy!

Flavor

"KEEP IT SIMPLE
TO KEEP IT REAL—
LESS IS ALMOST ALWAYS MORE!"

BROCCOLI SAUSAGE LINGUINE

NOTES FOR 4 SERVINGS

1/2 broccoli, cut into small florets
2 tbsp olive oil
A pat of butter
1 clove garlic, finely chopped
1/3 cup dry white wine
1 dried piri-piri chili, crushed
1 cup chicken stock
2 fennel or herb sausages
16 oz (1 package) linguine
Salt and freshly ground pepper

MUSIC

To make the sauce, steam the broccoli and set it aside. In a pan, heat the olive oil and the butter together over medium-high heat. Add the garlic and chili and sauté until golden. Pour in the white wine and reduce it by a third. Turn the heat up to high, add the chicken stock, and then reduce it by half. Add the steamed broccoli and mash it well, with a spoon. Take the pan off the heat and set aside. Slice open the sausages, remove the meat, and cook it in another pan. Add the cooked sausage and the cooking juices to the broccoli mixture, mix well, and season it generously with salt and pepper. Cook the linguine in salted water, drain it, and toss with the sauce. Serve in a warmed bowl and finish with more pepper.

3.25"

4.5"

BURGER WITH THE WORX

NOTES FOR 4 BURGERS

1 lb ground meat (veal, pork, or beef, or a mixture of the three)
1 egg
1 small onion, chopped
1 clove garlic, chopped
Salt and freshly ground pepper
3 oz pancetta or bacon
2 oz cream cheese
2 oz goat cheese
1 large onion, sliced
1 package mushrooms of your choice, sliced
2 tbsp olive oil
1 avocado, sliced
1 tomato, sliced
Dijon mustard
4 English muffins (or buns of your choice)

MUSIC

To make the patties, combine the ground meat, egg, and garlic in a bowl. Season the mixture with salt and pepper and shape it into 4 patties. Set aside. In a pan, or in the microwave, cook the pancetta or bacon until it's nice and crispy. Set aside. In a small bowl, combine the cream cheese and goat cheese into a smooth spread, and season it generously with pepper. In a pan over medium heat, sauté the sliced onion in 1 tbsp olive oil, until golden. Add the mushrooms and cook until golden. Season with salt and pepper and transfer to a bowl. In the same pan, heat the remaining olive oil and cook the patties however you like them: rare, medium, or—shudder to think—well done. To assemble the burgers, toast the English muffins. Spread 4 muffin halves with Dijon mustard and top each with some pancetta or bacon, a burger patty, a slice of tomato, a few slices of avocado, and 1 tbsp of the mushroom and onion mixture. Spread the other muffin halves with cheese spread, close the burgers, and dig in!

THIS RECIPE IS AN EXCELLENT SOURCE OF MEAT!

ANGRY PENNE

NOTES FOR 4 SERVINGS

2 tbsp olive oil
3 cloves garlic, chopped
2 dried piri-piri chilis, crushed
1 can (28 oz) whole Italian tomatoes
1 tsp salt
16 oz (1 package) penne rigate
A few leaves fresh basil, roughly chopped

MUSIC

To make the sauce, heat the olive oil in a pan over high heat. When the oil is hot, reduce the heat to medium and add the garlic and peppers. Sauté until the garlic is golden brown. Add the tomatoes and crush them with a spoon. Reduce the heat to medium-low and let the sauce simmer for 20 minutes. Add the salt only after the sauce has reduced. Cook the pasta in salted water according to the package directions, drain, and toss with the sauce. Serve in a warmed bowl, garnished with basil.

MATH FOR REBELS **101.1**

GINGER-LACQUERED SALMON

NOTES FOR 4 SERVINGS

1/4 cup Dijon mustard
3 tbsp soy sauce (sushi soy sauce, if you've got it)
3 tbsp fresh ginger, peeled and chopped
2 tbsp honey
1 tbsp vegetable oil
1/2 tsp sesame oil
4 salmon fillets (about 1/2 lb each)
Black sesame seeds, toasted

MUSIC

Preheat the oven to 375°F (190°C).
In a bowl, combine the mustard, soy sauce, ginger, honey, vegetable oil, and sesame oil. Pour the mixture over the salmon. Cook the fillets on a baking sheet lined with parchment paper for 7 to 12 minutes, depending on your oven and the thickness of the fillets, until the fish is opaque and flakes easily but is still slightly raw in the middle. Sprinkle with sesame seeds and serve with a side of sautéed bok choy or your favorite green veggies.

SERVED WITH BOK CHOY, THIS RECIPE IS AN EXCELLENT SOURCE OF BOK CHOY!

JAMAICAN CONE

NOTES FOR 6 SERVINGS

For the cones:
3 tbsp vegetable oil
3 boneless, skinless chicken breasts, cut into cubes
1 onion, thinly sliced
3 cloves garlic, chopped
2 large potatoes, finely diced
2 tbsp curry powder
3 carrots, grated
2 small fresh chili peppers of your choice, seeded and thinly sliced
4 cups chicken stock
Salt and freshly ground pepper
6 chapatis (Indian flatbreads)
Fresh cilantro, chopped

For the mango chutney:
1 tsp vegetable oil
2 tbsp butter
2 cloves garlic, finely chopped
1 ripe mango, cut into strips
3 tbsp sugar
Juice of 1 lime

MUSIC

For the cones: In a deep pot, brown the chicken in the vegetable oil. Add the onion and garlic and sauté over medium heat until the onion is translucent. Add the diced potatoes, curry powder, and carrots and mix well. Pour in the chicken stock and let it reduce until the potatoes are cooked and the mixture is thick. Season with salt and pepper to taste. For the chutney; In a small pot, sauté the garlic in the oil and butter. Add the mango, sugar, and lime juice and let the mixture reduce into a thick chutney, for about 10 minutes over low heat. To serve, roll the chapatis into cones and secure them with toothpicks. Warm them up in a 375°F (190°C) oven for 3 to 4 minutes and then transfer them to plates, stuff them with the chicken filling, and serve with mango chutney and fresh cilantro.

Tip: To serve, add a dash of piri-piri-style hot sauce to each cone and then crack open a few chilled Jamaican beers, like Carib!

GRILLED VEGGIE TOWER

NOTES FOR 4 SERVINGS

2 zucchinis, thinly sliced lengthwise
1 eggplant, sliced into rounds
2 roasted red peppers (roast them yourself and remove the skin, or use store-bought peppers in olive oil)
2 tbsp olive oil
1 egg yolk
1 clove garlic, crushed
1 tbsp lemon juice
Salt and freshly ground pepper
1/3 cup olive oil
1/4 cup fresh Parmesan cheese, grated
1 tsp anchovy paste
1 tbsp capers, chopped
3 oz goat cheese

MUSIC

Place the eggplant slices in a strainer and sprinkle them with salt to draw out the moisture. Let sit for 30 minutes. Rinse them quickly to remove the salt and dry well with paper towels. In a large bowl, combine the eggplant, zucchini, and 2 tbsp olive oil, and season with salt and pepper. Grill the veggies on the barbecue, or in a pan, until completely cooked and golden brown. Set aside. In another bowl, combine the egg yolk, garlic, lemon juice, and salt and pepper to taste. Add the 1/3 cup of olive oil in a slow, steady stream, whisking vigorously to create an emulsion, and then add the Parmesan, anchovy paste, and capers. To make the stack, use a round presentation ring or cookie cutter, or a ramekin. Start with a slice of grilled eggplant and then add zucchini, a slice of red pepper, and some goat cheese. Top with another eggplant round, another slice of zucchini, and finish with another slice of red pepper. Drizzle with the vinaigrette and repeat the process to make 4 stacks. Serve as an appetizer.

MANGO SHRIMP PINTXO

NOTES FOR 4 APPETIZERS

Around 20 fresh shrimp (big and juicy, none of those measly, flavorless frozen guys!), peeled
1 tbsp vegetable oil
2 cloves garlic, finely chopped
Juice of 1 lemon
Salad mix of your choice (like mesclun)
1 mango, thinly sliced
A few pinches black or white toasted sesame seeds

For the vinaigrette:
2 tbsp rice vinegar
2 tbsp honey
1 clove garlic, crushed
1 tsp Dijon mustard
1 tbsp fresh ginger, peeled and grated
1 tbsp sesame oil
6 tbsp vegetable oil

MUSIC

Marinate the shrimp in the oil, garlic, and lemon juice for 1 hour. Preheat the barbecue to 400°F (200°C). In a bowl, combine all the ingredients for the vinaigrette. Grill the shrimp on the barbecue for 5 to 7 minutes, watching them closely to make sure they don't overcook. To serve, toss the salad with a bit of vinaigrette and divide it between 4 bowls. Toss a handful of shrimp and a few mango slices into each bowl, drizzle the rest of the vinaigrette over top, and garnish with sesame seeds.

Tip: For a funkier presentation, thread the shrimp onto skewers, in a straight line from head to tail.

NOTES FOR 4 SERVINGS

1/2 cup 35% cream
1 tsp vanilla extract
3 ripe bananas
Store-bought tempura batter mix, prepared according to package directions

For the sauce:
3 oz dark rum
1/4 cup unsalted butter
1/4 cup cane sugar
2 tbsp 35% cream

For the garnish:
A handful of raisins or apricots

MUSIC

With a hand or stand mixer, whip the cream until stiff peaks form, about 3 to 5 minutes. Add the vanilla and refrigerate.

Preheat a fryer. Slice the bananas into thin rounds, dip them in the prepared tempura, and fry them in the fryer until golden brown. Meanwhile, heat all the sauce ingredients in a pot over medium-low heat, stirring constantly, until the sauce is thick and gooey. To serve, put the fried bananas into beautiful serving bowls, ladle a bit of sauce into each bowl, and top with whipped cream and dried fruit.

4PM / 7PM

QUESADILLAS DE LA MUERTE

NOTES FOR 4 SERVINGS

For the quesadillas:
3 tbsp olive oil
8 tortillas
2 cups cheddar cheese, grated
8 slices ham
1 avocado, thinly sliced
1 can (19 oz) red kidney beans, drained, rinsed, and puréed in a food processor
1/2 cup sour cream
1 lime

For the salsa:
2 big, fresh tomatoes, cut into cubes
1 cucumber, diced
1/2 cup fresh cilantro
1 clove garlic
1 shallot
1 tbsp honey
1 jalapeño pepper (or less, depending on how spicy you want your salsa to be), seeded
1 tbsp olive oil
Salt and freshly ground pepper

MUSIC

For the salsa, put all the ingredients into a food processor and pulse to finely chop, making sure not to purée. For the quesadillas, heat 1 tbsp of the olive oil in a pan. Put a tortilla into the pan and top it with 1/2 cup of cheddar cheese, 2 slices of ham, and a quarter of the sliced avocado. Spread a layer of bean purée on another tortilla and place it, purée side down, over the tortilla in the pan. Flip the quesadilla, adding just a bit more oil to the pan, and cook until the cheese is melted. Repeat with the remaining ingredients to make 4 quesadillas. Serve with sour cream, lime juice, and salsa.

SERRANO ASPARAGUS

NOTES FOR 4 SERVINGS

2 tbsp olive oil
1 tbsp balsamic vinegar
Salt to taste
Espelette pepper to taste
1 bunch asparagus, with the tough bottom ends trimmed off
Around 20 slices Serrano ham (Spanish ham)
Manchego cheese shavings

MUSIC

Preheat the oven to 400°F (200°C).
In a deep dish, combine the olive oil, balsamic vinegar, salt, Espelette pepper, and asparagus, and mix well to fully coat the asparagus in the dressing. Roll a slice of ham around each asparagus spear and arrange them on a baking sheet lined with parchment paper. Drizzle some more olive oil over the asparagus and cook for about 10 minutes, or until the asparagus are cooked but still crunchy. Transfer to a serving plate and top with Manchego cheese shavings.

BBQ CHICKEN À LA G

NOTES FOR 4 SERVINGS

8 boneless, skinless chicken thighs

For the marinade:
1/2 cup sushi soy sauce
1/2 cup honey
5 or 6 cloves garlic, crushed
3 tbsp sambal oelek

MUSIC

Combine all the marinade ingredients and marinate the chicken for 4 hours, or overnight.

Preheat the barbecue to 400°F (200°C).
Grill the chicken thighs over high heat for about 5 minutes with the barbecue cover open halfway, checking the chicken often. Flip the pieces, brush them with marinade, and continue cooking for a few more minutes.

Serve with basmati rice and/or sautéed bok choy.

AWESOME CALAMARI
WITH CILANTRO–LIME MAYO

NOTES FOR 2 APPETIZERS

For the mayonnaise:
1/2 cup mayonnaise
2 tbsp fresh cilantro, chopped
Juice of 1/2 lime
A small dollop of sambal oelek (to taste)

For the calamari:
6 whole squid, cleaned (tubes and tentacles)
1 cup milk
3 tbsp cornmeal
3 tbsp all-purpose flour
1 tsp garlic salt
1 tsp paprika
1 lemon

MUSIC

Preheat the fryer to 375°F (190°C).
For the mayonnaise, combine all the ingredients in a bowl and refrigerate. Slice the squid tubes into 1/2-inch rounds and soak them, along with the tentacles, in milk for 1 hour in the refrigerator. After 1 hour, drain the squid and dry them well with paper towels. In a large resealable plastic bag, combine the cornmeal, flour, garlic salt, and paprika. Transfer the squid to the bag and shake to fully coat. Fry the coated squid in the fryer until golden brown, about 2 minutes. Serve with lemon wedges and mayonnaise for dipping.

SPAGHETTI OF THE GODS

NOTES FOR 4 SERVINGS

5 tbsp olive oil
2 cloves garlic, roughly chopped
1 small onion, thinly sliced
1 small dried hot pepper, crushed (or crushed red pepper flakes to taste)
2 cups cherry tomatoes, halved
8 to 10 oz feta cheese, cut into small cubes (you can never have too much feta!)
3 cups fresh baby spinach
20 or so pitted Kalamata olives, halved
16 oz (1 package) long, thin pasta (angel hair pasta or spaghettini)

MUSIC

For the pasta, bring a large pot of salted water to a boil. In a deep pan or skillet, heat the olive oil over medium-high heat and sauté the garlic, onion, and hot pepper until the onion is translucent. Add the cherry tomatoes and cook over low heat for about 5 minutes. Meanwhile, cook the pasta according to the package directions. When the pasta is cooked, add it to the pan with the tomatoes, along with 1/2 cup of the pasta cooking water. Add the feta cheese, baby spinach, and olives. Give it a quick toss and then cover the pan for 2 minutes to wilt the spinach. Serve hot.

"ALWAYS EATING HEALTHY...
MAKES ME SICK!"

- The Rebel Chef

HUMMUS
NOTES

1 can (19 oz) chickpeas, drained and rinsed
1 tbsp tahini
3 tbsp olive oil
3 tbsp lemon juice
1 clove garlic, crushed
Salt and freshly ground pepper to taste
Paprika for garnish

MUSIC

In a food processor, purée all the hummus ingredients until smooth, except the paprika. Serve your hummus warm, garnished with a hefty splash of olive oil and sprinkled with paprika, with pita bread for dipping.

BABA GHANOUSH
NOTES

2 large eggplants
2 tbsp olive oil
Juice of 1 lemon
1 clove garlic, crushed
1/4 cup pine nuts
1/3 cup fresh Parmesan cheese, grated
Salt and freshly ground pepper to taste

MUSIC

Preheat the oven to 375°F (190°C).
Pierce the eggplant a few times with a fork and place on a baking sheet. Cook in the oven for about an hour, or until the flesh is cooked and tender. Let the eggplant cool slightly and then slice it lengthwise and scoop out the flesh. If needed, drain the flesh beforehand to remove any excess liquid. In a food processor, purée the eggplant, olive oil, lemon juice, garlic, pine nuts, and Parmesan cheese. Season with salt and pepper. Serve your baba ghanoush warm, decorated with pine nuts, with pita bread or fresh veggies for dipping.

Hummus

tip
Add turmeric, paprika, and cumin for irresistible color and flavor!

Baba ghanoush!

SUPPLÌ AL TELEFONO

RISOTTO ALLA MILANESE
NOTES

1 tsp saffron
1/2 cup white wine
1/4 cup butter
1 onion, finely chopped
16 oz Arborio rice
4 cups chicken stock
1-1/2 cups fresh Parmesan cheese, grated

MUSIC

In a small bowl, soak the saffron in the wine for 30 minutes. In a pot, melt the butter and cook the onions until translucent. Add the rice, saffron, and white wine, and stir continuously until the rice has absorbed all the liquid. Add the chicken stock one ladleful at a time, letting the rice absorb the stock before adding another ladleful. When all the liquid is absorbed and the rice is cooked, add the grated Parmesan cheese and mix well.

SUPPLÌ
NOTES FOR 4 SERVINGS

Chilled risotto alla milanese
3-1/2 oz mozzarella cheese, cut into cubes
3-1/2 oz prosciutto
A small bunch of fresh basil leaves
1 cup (250 ml) breadcrumbs

MUSIC

Preheat the fryer to 375°F (190°C).
Wrap each mozzarella cube in a small piece of prosciutto. With your hands, shape the risotto into 2-inch balls. Press a prosciutto-wrapped mozzarella cube and a small piece of basil into the center of each ball and seal the filling inside. Roll the balls in breadcrumbs and fry until golden brown (it should only take a few minutes). Serve for lunch with a green salad, or as an appetizer.

Supplì-me!

Italy!

LA polenta!

CAPONATA POLENTA

For the caponata:
1 eggplant, diced
2 zucchinis, diced
1 red pepper, diced
1 red onion, diced
2 tbsp capers
1/4 cup balsamic vinegar
1/4 cup olive oil
1 tsp sambal oelek
Salt and freshly ground pepper

2 cups homemade arrabbiata sauce (see Angry Penne on page 70 for the recipe)
1 roll store-bought polenta
1/2 cup fresh Parmesan cheese, grated
1/2 cup to 1 cup olive oil (enough to fill the pan with about 1/2 inch of oil)
A few leaves fresh basil for garnish (optional)

Preheat the oven to 375°F (190°C).
In a large bowl, combine the diced vegetables, capers, balsamic vinegar, olive oil, and sambal oelek. Season with salt and pepper. Spread the mixture evenly on a baking sheet lined with parchment paper and cook in the oven for about 50 minutes, stirring occasionally, until the vegetables are tender and slightly caramelized. Set aside. Heat the arrabbiata sauce in the microwave and set aside. Slice the polenta into 1/2-inch rounds and coat with Parmesan cheese. In a deep pan or skillet, fry the coated slices in olive oil on both sides, until golden brown. To serve, place 3 slices of polenta on each plate, top with 1/2 cup arrabbiata sauce, and finish with about 1/2 cup of caponata. Garnish with basil, if desired. Caponata on its own also makes a lip-smacking sauce!

BIG TUNA TARTARE

NOTES

12 oz sushi-quality red tuna
1/2 tsp sesame oil
1 tbsp sunflower or vegetable oil
1 tsp rice vinegar
1 tsp pickled ginger, finely chopped
2 avocados
1/2 tsp wasabi
1 tbsp lime juice
Salt and freshly ground pepper
A few pinches toasted black
and/or white sesame seeds

SERVES 4

MUSIC

Very finely dice the tuna and, in a bowl, combine it with the sesame oil, sunflower or vegetable oil, rice vinegar, and pickled ginger. Set aside. In another bowl, mash the avocados and add the lime juice and wasabi. Season with salt and pepper to taste.

Tip: To serve, I usually spoon a quarter of the avocado purée onto each plate and then top the avocado with a scoopful of tuna tartare. To finish, I just sprinkle the whole shebang with sesame seeds and wait for the compliments to start pouring in .

PORK ON FIRE

4 pork shoulder blade steaks, about 3/4 inch thick each

For the marinade:
3/4 cup extra-virgin or light olive oil
8 to 10 cloves garlic, crushed
2 tbsp crushed red pepper flakes
2 tbsp salt

MUSIC

Combine all the marinade ingredients and marinate the pork steaks for 4 hours, or overnight.

Preheat the barbecue to 400°F (200°C).
Sear the pork steaks on both sides to get some nice grill marks and then reduce the heat slightly so that the oil in the marinade doesn't catch fire. Cook the steaks on one side for about 6 to 8 minutes (until they have a really nice color), and then flip them and cook for another 4 or 5 minutes.

Serve with a crisp green salad.

7PM / 12AM

DIVINE PROFITEROLES

NOTES FOR 16 PROFITEROLES

6 tbsp milk
5 tbsp water
1/4 cup butter, softened
2/3 cup all-purpose flour
2 large eggs

1/2 cup good quality vanilla ice cream (or your favorite flavor!)
7 oz honey and almond nougat chocolate (like Toblerone®)
1/4 cup butter
1/4 cup 35% cream

MUSIC

Preheat the oven to 375°F (190°C).
Line a baking sheet with parchment paper, or with a silicone baking mat. To make the choux pastry, bring the milk, water, and butter to a boil over medium heat. Once the mixture starts to bubble, take the pot off the heat and add the flour all at once. Mix vigorously and then return the pot to the stovetop. Cook, stirring constantly, until the pastry pulls away from the sides and bottom of the pot. Take the pot off the heat again and let the pastry cool until warm. Add the eggs, one at a time, mixing well after each addition. Spoon the pastry into a pastry bag fitted with a round tip (or a resealable plastic bag with one end snipped off) and pipe the dough into 16 evenly-sized balls on the baking sheet. Bake for about 20 minutes, or until the pastry is puffed up and golden. Cool on a wire baking rack, so that they don't go soggy.

In a small pot, melt the butter, chocolate, and cream over low heat. Set aside.

When you're ready to serve the profiteroles, cut the puffs in half and top each base with a small scoop of vanilla ice cream. Replace the tops to make tiny sandwiches, transfer to plates, and ladle as much chocolate sauce as you want over them. I dare you to eat just one!

OLGA'S TARTIFLETTE

NOTES FOR 4 BIG HELPINGS

4 large potatoes, peeled and sliced into 1/2-inch rounds
1 cup lardons or thick-cut smoked bacon, diced
1 large onion, sliced
1-1/2 cups dry white wine
2 tbsp 35% cream
1 Reblochon cheese, sliced horizontally to make 2 rounds
Salt and freshly ground pepper

MUSIC

Preheat the oven to 350°F (175°C).
Boil the potatoes until just tender (if the potatoes are overcooked, they'll be mushy and fall apart). Set the potatoes aside and, in a pan, sauté the lardons or bacon until golden brown. Add the onion and cook until translucent. Add the wine and potatoes and let the wine reduce without stirring, to prevent the potatoes from breaking. When the liquid is reduced, season with salt and pepper to taste. Carefully transfer the mixture to an oven-safe dish, pour the cream over all, and top with the Reblochon, rind up. Bake for 25 minutes, until the cheese is melted, bubbly, and lightly golden. If you want to go the whole hog, fry the potatoes in butter until golden brown before adding them to the bacon and onion mixture.

Serve with a green salad… just kidding!

YOUR DAILY DOSE OF DELICIOUS CHEESE!

FISH IN A PIG

NOTES FOR 3 SERVINGS

1 pork loin
1 skinless trout fillet
2 shallots, finely chopped
1 tsp fennel seeds
1 tsp fresh or dried dill
1 tbsp lemon juice
1 tbsp olive oil
Salt and freshly ground pepper
A bit of olive oil
1 bulb fennel, thinly sliced (about 1/4 inch thick)
2 oz pastis
1/3 cup chicken stock
A bit of lemon juice

MUSIC

Preheat the oven to 375°F (190°C).

Butterfly the pork loin by carefully slicing along the side horizontally, without separating it completely. Open the loin like a book and then pound it with a kitchen mallet or a rolling pin until it's fairly thin. Spread a quarter of the shallots over top, along with the fennel seeds and dill. Cut the trout fillet in half lengthwise to make 2 narrow fillets and place them, lengthwise and one on top of the other, in the middle of the pork loin. Pour the lemon juice and the 1 tbsp olive oil over the fish and season with salt and pepper. Fold the pork around the fish to make a log and tie it securely with kitchen string. Heat a pan over high heat. Oil the outside of the meat and sear it on all sides. Transfer it to a baking dish and bake for 20 to 25 minutes. While the meat is cooking, evenly spread the fennel on a baking sheet, drizzle it with oil, and season it with salt and pepper. Put it in the oven about 10 minutes before the meat is done.

To make the sauce, put the pan used to sear the meat back on the stovetop and deglaze it with the pastis, scraping up all the tasty bits stuck to the bottom of the pan. When the pastis has reduced by half, add the chicken stock and reduce it by half again. Add the remaining shallots and a good squeeze of lemon juice. Season with salt and pepper to taste. Slice up the meat and serve it over a bed of roasted fennel and a ton of tasty sauce.

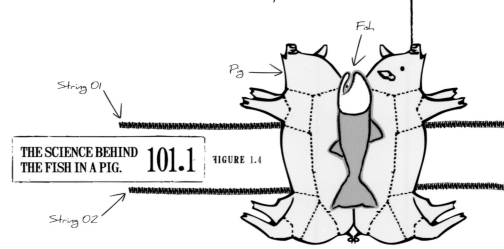

THE SCIENCE BEHIND THE FISH IN A PIG. **101.1** FIGURE 1.4

FIGURE 1.4

DIABLO CHICKEN

NOTES FOR 4 SERVINGS

8 chicken drumsticks, with skin
12 chicken wings
1 tbsp garlic salt
1 tbsp poultry seasoning
1 tbsp paprika
3 tbsp piri-piri sauce
3 tbsp Portuguese hot pimento paste
2 tbsp olive oil
1 clove garlic, chopped

The Secret Weapon.

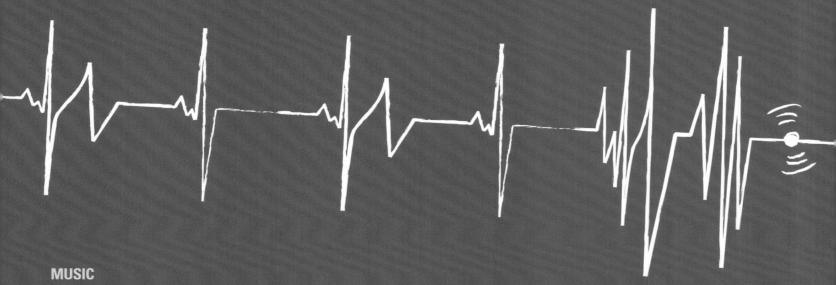

MUSIC

Preheat the oven to 400°F (200°C).
In a large bowl, combine the chicken drumsticks, chicken wings, garlic salt, poultry seasoning, and paprika and mix well. Transfer the chicken to a baking sheet and cook for 20 minutes. Flip the wings and cook for another 20 minutes. Remove the wings and cook the drumsticks for 20 minutes longer (for a total cooking time of 1 hour). If you want to cut down on fat, cook the chicken on a grill rack over a baking sheet.

Preheat the barbecue to 400°F (200°C).
In a small bowl, combine the piri-piri sauce, hot pimento paste, olive oil, and garlic. Brush the chicken with the sauce and cook for 20 minutes, flipping it halfway through.

Tip: This chicken is WICKEDLY spicy! For a milder version, cut back on the piri-piri sauce. Piri-piri sauce and Portuguese hot pimento paste can be found in most supermarkets and in Portuguese specialty stores. Serve with ice-cold beer!

SCALOPINE AL LIMONE

NOTES FOR 4 SERVINGS

4 large veal cutlets
Salt and freshly ground pepper
1 tbsp olive oil
2 tbsp butter
1/2 cup white wine
1 cup chicken stock
2 tbsp capers
2 tbsp lemon juice
Chopped fresh parsley for garnish

MUSIC

Season the veal cutlets with salt and pepper. In a pan, heat the oil and butter over high heat and cook the cutlets for about 1 minute on each side. Set aside. In the same pan, reduce the white wine until about 2 to 3 tbsp remain. Add the chicken stock and reduce by half. Chop 1-1/2 tbsp of the capers and add them to the pan with the remaining whole capers. Add the lemon juice, transfer the cutlets back to the pan, and cook them for around a minute to reheat. Adjust the seasoning, sprinkle with parsley, and serve!

Creole Pork

NOTES FOR 4 SERVINGS

1 pork loin
2 tsp lemon pepper
Salt
2 tbsp olive oil
2 tbsp lemon juice
1 tbsp Worcestershire sauce
1 tbsp Dijon mustard
2 tbsp shallots, chopped
1 tsp sambal oelek

MUSIC

Cut the pork loin into 1-inch slices and sprinkle with lemon pepper and salt. In a pan over medium heat, heat the olive oil and cook the pork until golden brown, about 3 to 4 minutes. Transfer the pork to a serving plate and set aside. In the same pan used to brown the pork, cook the lemon juice, Worcestershire sauce, Dijon, and sambal oelek together for 2 to 3 minutes. Stir in the chopped shallots and then pour the sauce over the pork. Serve with your favorite veggies on the side.

PAPRIKA LIME ROAST CHICKEN

For the marinade:
1/2 cup olive oil
3 tbsp paprika
3 tbsp chili powder (or sambal oelek)
3 tbsp salt

For the chicken:
1 medium chicken
5 limes, quartered
8 new potatoes, cut into fairly thin wedges
Sliced pancetta, rolled (optional)

MUSIC

Two hours before your serious hunger kicks in, combine all the marinade ingredients. It should have the consistency of a thick paste; if it's too watery, add more paprika. Season generously with salt.

Split the chicken by cutting down the back, along the spine, with kitchen scissors or a large, sharp knife. Slide your fingers under the skin of the breasts, legs, and wings to separate it from the meat, but leave the skin on. Spread the marinade between the skin and the meat. Try to get it into every nook and cranny, for maximum flavor! Brush the underside of the chicken with the rest of the marinade and then let it marinate in the refrigerator for 1 hour.

Preheat the oven to 350°F (175°C).
Place the split chicken, meat side up, in a large baking dish or pan, directly on top of 4 quartered limes. Arrange the new potatoes around the chicken and squeeze the juice of the remaining lime over everything. If you really want to go all out, tuck rolled pancetta slices between the potatoes.

Bake for 45 minutes and then check the chicken for doneness. If the chicken isn't totally cooked, cook for 15 minutes longer. The legs should pull away easily, and the potatoes should be golden brown.

Tip: If you can find dried (black) limes, use them instead of the fresh limes under the chicken to add complexity to the citrusy tang!

STEAK WITH CALVADOS CREAM

NOTES FOR 4 SERVINGS

For the marinade:
1 beef flank steak (between 1-1/2 and 2 lbs)
3 tbsp olive oil
3 tbsp Dijon mustard
1 tsp *herbes de Provence*

For the sauce:
3 oz calvados (or your favorite brandy)
2 tbsp Worcestershire sauce
1 clove garlic, crushed
1 tbsp Dijon mustard
3/4 cup 35% cream
Salt and freshly ground pepper

MUSIC

The night before, place the steak in a dish, or in a large resealable plastic bag, and add the olive oil, Dijon, and *herbes de Provence*. Mix well to coat and then refrigerate overnight. To cook the meat, preheat the oven to 200°F (90°C). Using a fork, scrape the marinade off the meat and then, with a knife, score the steak in a diamond pattern on both sides. Heat a pan over high heat, sear it on both sides, and then transfer it to a baking pan and cook it in the oven until the meat's internal temperature reaches 137°F (58°C). Remove the steak from the oven, cover it with aluminum foil, and let it rest for 10 minutes. While the meat is resting, heat the pan used to sear the meat and **deglaze** it with the calvados, scraping up the flavorful bits stuck to the bottom of the pan. Let the calvados reduce by two thirds. Add the Worcestershire sauce, garlic, mustard, and cream and bring the sauce to a boil. Lower the heat and let the sauce simmer for 3 minutes. Season with salt and pepper. Cut the steak into thin slices, about 1/4 inch thick each, and serve smothered in sauce, with roasted vegetables or salad.

Tip: Your sauce will be even tastier if you add the steak juices from the pan!

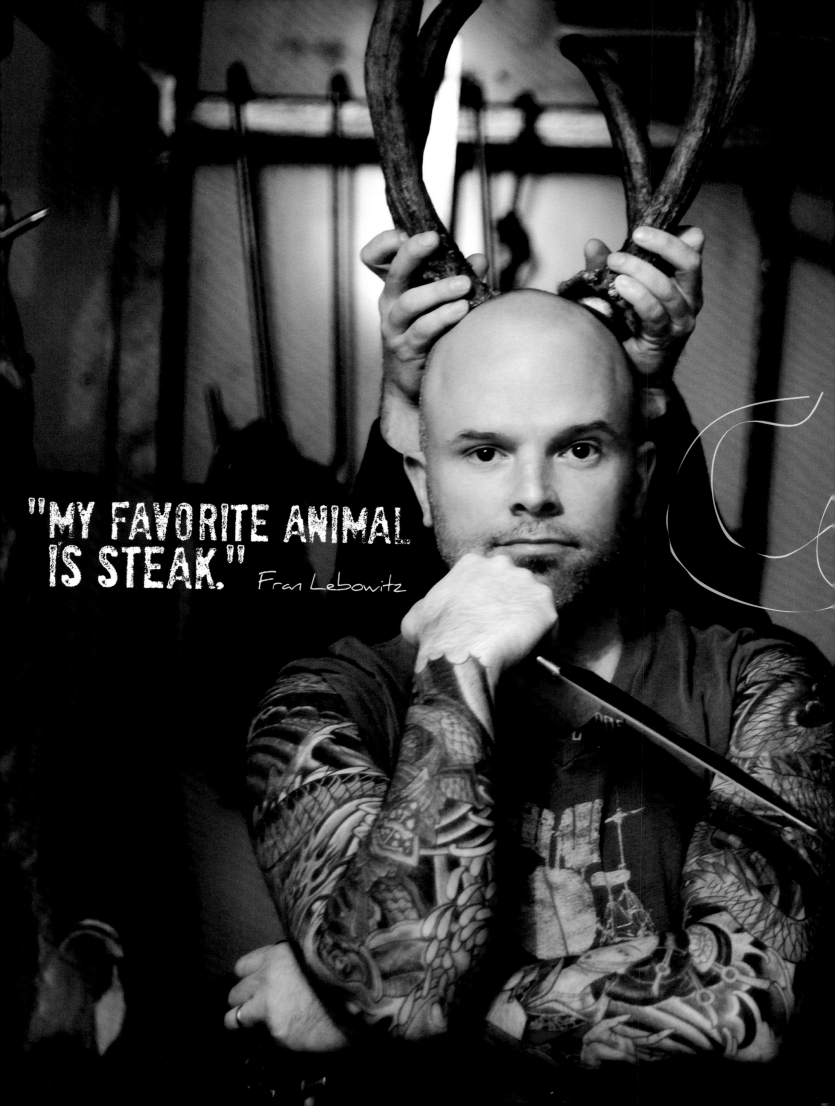

"MY FAVORITE ANIMAL IS STEAK." Fran Lebowitz

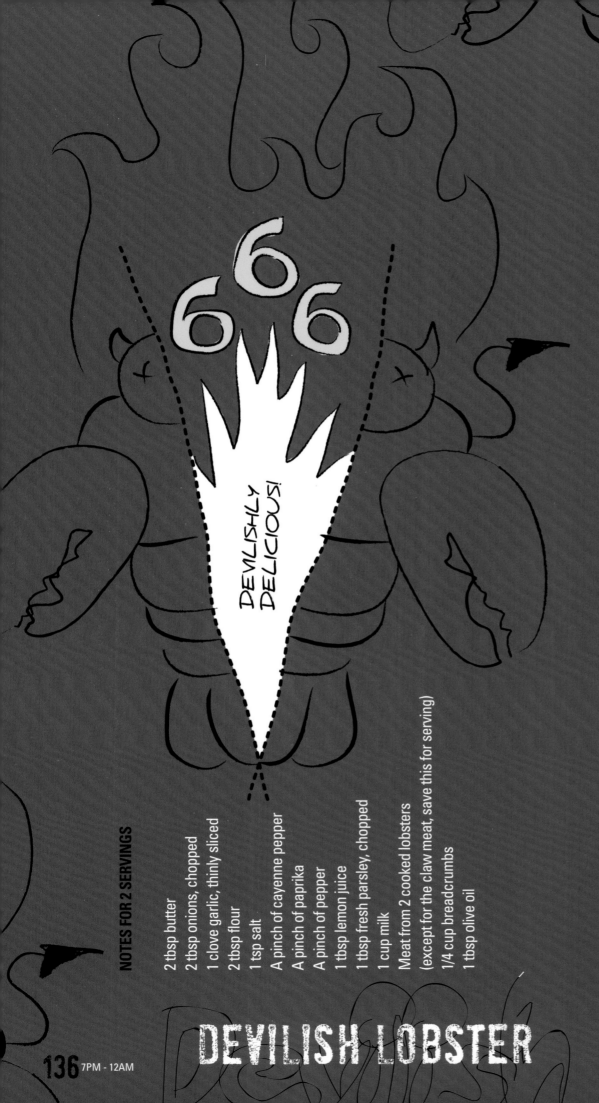

666

DEVILISHLY DELICIOUS!

NOTES FOR 2 SERVINGS

2 tbsp butter
2 tbsp onions, chopped
1 clove garlic, thinly sliced
2 tbsp flour
1 tsp salt
A pinch of cayenne pepper
A pinch of paprika
A pinch of pepper
1 tbsp lemon juice
1 tbsp fresh parsley, chopped
1 cup milk
Meat from 2 cooked lobsters
(except for the claw meat, save this for serving)
1/4 cup breadcrumbs
1 tbsp olive oil

MUSIC

In a deep pan, heat the butter over medium heat and sauté the onions and garlic. Add the flour, salt, cayenne pepper, paprika, pepper, lemon juice, and parsley and mix well. Pour in the milk and cook, stirring constantly, until the mixture thickens.

Stir in the lobster meat.

To finish this dish, I fill the emptied and cleaned lobster shells with the mixture, sprinkle it with breadcrumbs and a good drizzle of olive oil, and broil the stuffed shells until the breadcrumbs are golden brown. Serve with the lobster claws.

DEVILISH LOBSTER

ITALIAN MAKI

NOTES FOR 4 SERVINGS

For the sauce:
2 tbsp olive oil
3 cloves garlic, finely chopped
1 small dried hot pepper, crushed
1 can (28 oz) whole or diced Italian tomatoes
Salt and freshly ground pepper

For the chicken maki:
4 chicken breast cutlets
8 slices prosciutto
16 asparagus spears, blanched
8 slices mozzarella cheese
2 tbsp olive oil
3 tbsp Marsala (or white wine)
1/4 cup chicken stock

MUSIC

For the tomato sauce, heat the olive oil and sauté the garlic and hot pepper until the garlic is lightly golden. Add the tomatoes and crush them with a spoon. Reduce the sauce by half and season with salt and pepper. Set aside. To make the chicken maki, pound the chicken cutlets with a kitchen mallet until fairly thin and then top each cutlet with 2 slices of prosciutto, 4 asparagus spears (leave 2 tips poking out on each side), and 2 slices of mozzarella. Roll the chicken around the fillings and tie with kitchen string, or close with toothpicks. In a pan, heat the olive oil over high heat and sear the rolls on all sides, until golden brown. Lower the heat and cook until the meat is no longer pink inside. Remove the rolls from the pan and set aside. Deglaze the same pan with the Marsala and reduce by half. Add the chicken stock and reduce by half again. To serve, slice each roll into 6 pieces, arrange over a pool of tomato sauce, and ladle the Marsala sauce generously over top.

Tip: To save time, make the sauce up to two days in advance.

Boucherie Les Épicurieux
Montreal

GAME WITH WILD MUSHROOM SAUCE

A_1

Antoine Sicotte

CARNIVORE

NOTES FOR 4 SERVINGS

1 cup fresh, or 1/2 oz dried chanterelle mushrooms
(or use any fresh wild mushrooms that are in season)
1 tbsp duck fat (or vegetable oil, if you don't have duck fat)
4 shallots, thinly sliced
1/4 cup white wine
A pinch of pepper
A pinch of nutmeg
1/4 cup fresh parsley, chopped
1 lb ground pork
4 venison steaks (or any other meat of your choice), pounded into thin cutlets
4 strips of pork fat (or 4 large, thin carrot strips)
A bit more duck fat or oil
2 shallots, thinly sliced
1/2 oz dried morel mushrooms (or use 1 cup of any fresh wild mushrooms that are in season)
Salt and freshly ground pepper
1/4 cup 35% cream (optional)

MUSIC

Preheat the oven to 350°F (180°C).
If you're using dried chanterelles, soak them in 1/2 cup cold water for 15 minutes, or according to the package directions.

In a pan, heat the duck fat over medium-high heat and sauté the shallots and chanterelles. When the shallots are nice and soft, deglaze the pan with white wine. Add the pepper, nutmeg, and parsley and let simmer for a few minutes to reduce the wine. In a bowl, combine the pork and the shallot and mushroom mixture and shape it into 4 equal balls. Spread the venison steaks out flat and put a pork ball in the center of each steak, and then roll the steaks around the pork and wrap to close. Wrap a strip of pork fat (or carrot) around each roll and tie securely with kitchen string. Sear the meat in the same pan used to cook the shallots and chanterelles, transfer to a baking pan, and cook in the oven for about 40 minutes, or until the pork stuffing is fully cooked. Meanwhile, soak the dried morels in 1/2 cup water for 15 minutes. Sauté the 2 thinly sliced shallots in the duck fat or oil. When the shallots are soft, add the morels along with the soaking liquid. Let it reduce to the thickness you prefer, and then season with salt and pepper to taste. Serve the meat smothered in sauce, with whichever side dish you feel goes best with this succulent dish!

Tip: For a sinfully rich sauce, my butcher, Mario, always adds 1/4 cup 35% cream before reducing!

BLACK AND BLUE PASTA

NOTES FOR 4 SERVINGS

1/2 cup chicken stock
1/2 cup 35% cream
4 oz blue cheese
4 oz cream cheese
1 tsp freshly ground pepper
1 package (16 oz) cuttlefish or squid ink pasta
1/2 cup pine nuts, toasted
1 red pepper, finely chopped

CUTTLEFISH
The cuttlefish is related to the squid, and its ink has a subtle flavor and super intense color.

What the @#!% is cuttlefish?

MUSIC

In a pan over high heat, reduce the chicken stock and cream by half. Lower the heat to medium and then add the blue cheese, cream cheese, and pepper, and stir until both cheeses are melted. Cook the pasta in salted water. Add the cooked pasta and the pine nuts to the sauce (save a few pine nuts for serving), and toss to coat. Serve the pasta topped with pine nuts and red pepper.

Tip: Toast the pine nuts in a pan, without oil, until golden brown. Keep a close eye on them to make sure they don't burn!

VINS AUX VERRES

BLANCS

Casa de Mouraz '04 .... 5.75
Pays Portugal
Jacob's Creek '07 .... 6.00
Sémillon-Chardonnay
Alisoté "Les Terperreex" ... 7.50
Riesling Réserve '09 ...... 8.00
Pinot Grigio DJ, Vénétie ... 8.25
Muscadet Sèvre & Maine 8.50
Sur lie 2006, Pernaud
Sauvignon Blanc, NZ 8.50
Kim Crawford 08
Chardonnay Sterling 06 .... 9.00
Riesling Fallen Angel, NZ .. 11.00
Bourgogne Marqués de 11.25
Mac Mahon, 2005
Sancerre Elégance '07 ..... 11.75
Chablis '06, J.P.A Ellevin . 12.00

ROUGES

Cuspide 2006, Espagne 6.50
Jacob's Creek 2006 .... 7.00
Shiraz, Cabernet
Merlot 2005 Sterling 8.25
Cab.-Sauvignon "Chocolan" . 8.25
Malbec "Punto Final" '06 .. 8.50
Pinot Noir Brancott, ... 8.75
Nouvelle Zélande 2007
Côtes du Rhône '04, Guigal . 9.00
Zinfandel, Tamas Estate ... 9.25
1ères Côtes de Blaye '05 .. 9.25
ch Frédignac
Madiran '05 Paradilys 9.50
Brouilly 2006, P.A Dumas .. 10.00

CHIVAS

COUNTRY STEW

NOTES FOR 4 SERVINGS

1 pork loin

Salt and freshly ground pepper

3 tbsp olive oil

4 sausages (spicy or mild Italian, or Toulouse)

2 large onions, chopped

3 cloves garlic, chopped

1 cup white wine

1 cup chicken stock

8 fresh Italian (Roma) tomatoes, diced

2 bay leaves

5 leaves fresh sage, chopped

3 tbsp fresh parsley, chopped

MUSIC

Season the pork loin with salt and pepper. Oil the meat with 1 tbsp olive oil and sear it in a deep pot or Dutch oven over high heat. When the pork is nice and golden brown, remove it from the pan and set aside. Add the remaining 2 tbsp olive oil to the pot and sauté the onions and garlic over medium heat for 3 minutes. Add the white wine and whole sausages and let simmer until only about 1/4 cup of the liquid remains. Add the chicken stock, tomatoes, bay leaves, and sage. Return the pork loin to the pot and let it all simmer for about 20 minutes, or until the pork is just slightly pink in the center. Remove the pork and sausages and cut into 1-inch slices. Arrange the sliced meat in a deep serving dish and pour the sauce over all. Sprinkle with parsley and serve with green beans sautéed in butter and garlic.

Tip: Meat has to be seared over really high heat, so to prevent the oil from burning it's best to rub it directly onto the meat instead of pouring it into the pan.

RACK OF LAMB
WITH HERB CRUST

NOTES FOR 4 SERVINGS

1/4 cup breadcrumbs
3 tbsp fresh thyme, chopped
3 tbsp fresh rosemary, chopped
2 tbsp fresh chives, finely chopped
2 cloves garlic, finely chopped
7 tbsp olive oil
1 tsp Espelette pepper
A pinch of salt
2 racks of lamb
Salt and freshly ground pepper

MUSIC

Preheat the oven to 375°F (190°C).
In a bowl, combine all the ingredients, except the racks of lamb. Set the mixture aside. Season the racks of lamb with salt and pepper and sear them in a pan over high heat for 2 to 3 minutes. Take the lamb out of the pan and spread a layer of the breadcrumb mixture over the top of each rack. Transfer to a roasting pan, bone sides down, and cook in the oven for 15 to 20 minutes, depending on the degree of doneness that you want. Slice up each rack, cutting between the bones, and serve with rosemary potatoes and seasonal vegetables.

Tip: Your best bet for testing the lamb for doneness is to use a meat thermometer. It makes all the difference between a rack of lamb that's nice and pink and lamb that's still alive!

AN EXCELLENT SOURCE
OF LAMB!

FUNKY CHORIZO

NOTES

3 tbsp olive oil
3 cloves garlic, roughly chopped
4 large slices 2-day-old country bread, cut into cubes
1/2 lb chorizo, cut into 1/2-inch slices
1/3 lb whole olives in oil (not the small pimento-stuffed olives!)
2 tsp fresh parsley, chopped
Paprika

MUSIC

In a pan, heat the olive oil and add the garlic and cubed bread, and cook until the bread is golden brown. Add the chorizo and olives and sauté for about 2 minutes.

Tip: I serve this as an appetizer, sprinkled with parsley and paprika.

NORTH AFRICAN
TAGINE

NOTES FOR 6 SERVINGS

2-1/4 lbs lamb shoulder, cubed
2 onions, chopped
3 cloves garlic, crushed
3 tbsp olive oil
1 tsp ground ginger
1 tsp cumin
1 tsp paprika
1 tsp turmeric
Freshly ground pepper to taste
1 can (28 oz) tomatoes
2 cinnamon sticks
1 lb prunes
2 tbsp honey
Salt
1 cup blanched almonds, toasted
A handful of fresh mint and fresh cilantro

SERVES 6

MUSIC

Soak the prunes in a bowl of water for 6 hours to rehydrate them.

In another bowl, toss the cubed lamb with the onions, garlic, olive oil, ginger, cumin, paprika, and turmeric. Season generously with pepper, cover, and let it marinate for at least 2 hours.

Remove the lamb from the marinade, reserving the marinade for the sauce. In a deep pot, sauté the lamb in a bit of oil until the cubes are golden brown. Add the leftover marinade, along with the tomatoes and cinnamon sticks, and let simmer, covered, for 1-1/2 hours. Meanwhile, heat the drained prunes and honey in a small pot, adding just enough water to cover the prunes, and let simmer for 10 minutes. About 10 minutes before taking the lamb off the heat, add the prunes and their liquid and cook for the last 10 minutes. Salt to taste.

Tip: Serve over couscous, with the blanched almonds and fresh mint and cilantro.

Moroccan mint tea

To make authentic Moroccan tea, first pour a bit of boiling water over a bit of gunpowder tea and let it steep for a minute to remove the bitterness. Strain the tea, discard the water, and add more water and a handful of mint leaves, making sure the mint leaves are completely covered in water (the leaves will have a bitter taste, what the Moroccans call "burnt tea," if they're in contact with the air while brewing). Add sugar and drink up!

tip!

GORGEOUS GARLIC ROASTED POTATOES

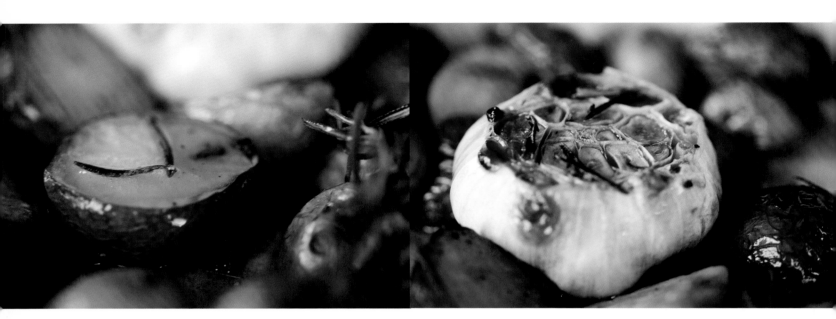

NOTES FOR 6 SERVINGS

2 whole heads garlic
About 1-1/2 lbs new potatoes, halved
1/4 cup olive oil
Salt and freshly ground pepper
3 sprigs fresh rosemary or 1 tbsp dried rosemary

MUSIC

Preheat the oven to 400°F (200°C).
With a knife, cut off the tops of the garlic heads to expose the tops of the cloves. In a large bowl, toss the garlic heads with the potatoes and olive oil. Crush the sprigs of rosemary with the blade of a knife to release the oils, and add to the potatoes. Mix well and season with salt and pepper to taste. Roast the potatoes in the oven for 45 minutes, or until golden brown, stirring every 15 minutes. Serve as a side dish with meat.

VEGGIE CANNELLONI

NOTES FOR 4 SERVINGS

1 tbsp olive oil
4 cloves garlic
4 shallots, roughly chopped
1-1/2 cups store-bought roasted red peppers, drained
1/2 cup chicken stock
2 eggplants, cut lengthwise into 1/2-inch-thick slices
1/2 cup goat cheese
1/4 cup Kalamata olives, pitted and chopped
1 tbsp capers, chopped
2 tbsp fresh parsley, chopped
Fresh Parmesan cheese, grated
Salt and freshly ground pepper

MUSIC

Preheat the oven to 400°F (200°C).

In a pan over medium heat, heat the olive oil and sauté the garlic and shallots for 1 minute. Reduce the heat and cook for another 3 minutes, until golden brown. Add the roasted peppers and chicken stock, season with pepper, and cook for 5 more minutes. Let the mixture cool and then purée in a food processor until smooth. Brush the eggplant slices with olive oil. Transfer them to a baking sheet and cook in the oven for 15 minutes. In a bowl, mix together the cheese, olives, capers, and 1 tbsp (15 ml) of the parsley. Spread 1 tbsp of this mixture onto each cooked eggplant slice, roll them up carefully, and cook them in the oven for another 15 minutes. Ladle a bit of sauce onto each serving plate and top each pool with an eggplant cannelloni. Sprinkle with Parmesan cheese

WHISKEY COLA SORBET

NOTES FOR 4 SERVINGS

2-1/2 oz whiskey (or rum)
2-1/2 cups flat cola
1/2 cup sugar

MUSIC

In a small pot, heat the whiskey over medium heat for 2 or 3 minutes. Add the cola and sugar and continue heating the mixture until the sugar is dissolved. Take the pot off the heat and chill it in the refrigerator until cool. When the syrup is nice and cold, pour it into an ice cream maker and freeze for 20 minutes, according to the manufacturer's directions. For harder sorbet, freeze it in the freezer until you're ready to serve.

TIRAMISU

NOTES

4 eggs, separated
3/4 cup sugar
14 oz mascarpone cheese
7 oz ladyfinger cookies
3/4 cup strong espresso
3 tbsp hazelnut liqueur (like Frangelico)
Chocolate, grated

MUSIC

In a bowl, using a hand or stand mixer, whip the egg whites until stiff peaks form. In another bowl, beat the egg yolks and the sugar until thick and pale. Carefully fold in the mascarpone cheese and then the egg whites. In a small bowl, combine the coffee and hazelnut liqueur. To assemble the tiramisu, quickly dip each ladyfinger in the coffee and liqueur mixture. Arrange soaked ladyfingers in a serving dish, enough to cover the bottom. Spread half of the mascarpone mixture over the ladyfingers, and then top with another layer of soaked cookies. Finish with another layer of the mascarpone mixture, and then refrigerate for at least 4 hours.

Sprinkle with chocolate right before serving.

Notes

Notes

Notes

RECIPE INDEX

Acknowledgments

First, I'd like to thank my editor Richard Trempe, without whom this book would never have seen the light of day.

A huge thank you to my two partners in crime in this rebel endeavor: Antoine Ross Trempe from Cardinal Publishers and Albert Elbilia, photographer and art director extraordinaire. Antoine, thank you for your support, your creativity, your strength when times were tough, and most especially for your way with words. Albert, you are a true artist; thank you for sharing your passion with me, and for the hard work and long hours you put into this book, as if it were your own.

Thank you to my father for his recipes and his collaboration, but most of all, for passing his love of food on to me.

Thank you to Joé, my love, who rode with me through the ups and downs of the roller-coaster of emotions I went through while working on this project, and who has stuck by my side year after year.

Thank you to my friends and family for their comments and suggestions throughout the entire process.

Thank you to Simon Laplante and Maurice Holder from Chez Holder.

Thank you to Mario, Pascal, and Joanne from the Les Épicurieux butcher shop. Thanks to the fine folks at Café Italia, Boulangerie Marguerita, Épicerie Benfeito, and Milano.

I'd also like to give a shout out to Tattoomania.

And of course, thank you, reader!